It Comes In Waves

Elle Marie

BookLeaf
Publishing

Presentation by *BookLeaf Publishing*

Web: www.bookleafpub.com

E-mail: info@bookleafpub.com

ISBN: 9789357619486

First edition 2022

Escape

I want to escape to the middle of our novel
Frolic in the memories
And for just a moment...
forget how the story ends.

Dive

Dive
Dive deep into the depths of my soul
Dance with my darkness as you divulge your own
Tell me what sparks a fire in your soul and the things that have broken your spirit
Be unapologetically yourself for just a moment in time.
Just feel...
Life is too short not to feel
Alive.

Crumbs

I'm the love of your life
but nothing is ever enough
showered me with affection
now all you leave is crumbs
I'm perfect in every way
but undeserving of such love
I've been depleted and exhausted by you
but yet
I feel too much…

Shatter

Broken shards of glass
bleeding hands
Gathered and glued
Fragile and beautiful
You memorized the weak spots
discovered all the cracks
You knew exactly where to press to watch it all
crumble
I gave you my trust
And you used it…
To Shatter me

Deceitful

One Lie off your lips was enough to create doubt
in a million truths.

Foundation

Collapsed my home
While building yours
Constructed until you were
Complete
Used my own foundation
To lay your bricks
All the while
I was weakening my home
betraying myself…
destroying myself…
to build your house

…

and you locked me out.

Destruction

loving you was the
most beautiful arrangement
of self- destruction.

Betrayal

You mirrored my darkness
The fears deep inside
heightened emotions
fragility I hide
Betrayal courses through my veins
Brewing up a storm
But I refuse to set myself on fire
Just to keep you warm.

Shallow

You may think she's pretty on the outside, but
have you looked within?
Have you tried to explore the inner workings of
her mind?
What makes her tick?
Considered diving deep into the magic of her
soul?
What inspires her to keep going?
How about the beauty and pain that lies deep
within her heart?
No, my dear, you have only grazed the surface.
You prefer to wade in shallow water because
depth frightens you.
Good thing.
Because you might drown.

Venom

Falling in love with
potential
is a lingering poison.

Home

Like a familiar story
I know every part of you
The warmness
The comfort
The feeling of home
So easily I tumble back to the comfort in reading
you over again
Skimming over the chapters that I do not want to
revisit
pretending that they don't exist.
nevertheless… One flawed chapter doesn't mean
the story is over, does it?
all you have to do is turn the page…

Narcissist

The only way to win
is
to no longer play
…
Loving a narcissist

Forgiveness

Sweet girl,
Forgive yourself.
Forgive yourself for each time you settled for
less than you deserved.
Forgive yourself for each time you tried over
again only to leave with bleeding hands and a
broken heart.
Forgive yourself because this world is not meant
for a love like yours.
Forgive yourself but never stop
Loving
There is no doubt that the world needs more of
it.

Powerful

In the stillness of the silence you called for me
Asking me to come back home
Remember who you are you whispered
But…I'm not her anymore
No, my darling
you're not
you are *so* much stronger.

Indestructible

Collect those tiny fragments of glass broken off
the bedroom floor
Those shattered thoughts and pieces of love once
lost
Glue them back together into a kaleidoscope of
beauty
It's time to love yourself again.

Sanctuary

Blank sheets of paper
Caressed with black ink
My safe space
For emotions to flow
You listen to my words
That I cannot voice
and turn my pain
Into
something *beautiful.*

Almost

one day, perhaps
a love will come
to not only relish my sunlight
but my storms as well

…
We were so close

Spring

And there you stood
A glimmer of sunshine after a long winter
A warm breeze after the melting of the last frost
The beginning of a new life
The promise of spring.

You

And somewhere In between
The magic of friendship and love
Was you.

Future

I found you
Amidst the chaos of life
Among the noise of a million racing thoughts
and a hundred why nots…
There was one what if?

Time

Like an old book she visited her memories
Running her hands down the well-worn pages.
She paused a moment just to revel in the
familiarity of it.
She smiled
then slowly closed the book.
She knew how it ended.
And now…
Its time to write a new story.

Printed in the USA
CPSIA information can be obtained
at www.ICGtesting.com
LVHW020549221223
767112LV00093B/4833